OXFORD
First Book
of
Dinosaurs

Barbara Taylor

OXFORD
UNIVERSITY PRESS

OXFORD
UNIVERSITY PRESS

Great Clarendon Street, Oxford OX2 6DP

Oxford University Press is a department of the University of Oxford.
It furthers the University's objective of excellence in research, scholarship,
and education by publishing worldwide in

Oxford New York

Athens Auckland Bangkok Bogotá Buenos Aires
Cape Town Chennai Dar es Salaam Delhi Florence Hong Kong Istanbul
Karachi Kolkata Kuala Lumpur Madrid Melbourne Mexico City Mumbai
Nairobi Paris São Paulo Shanghai Singapore Taipei Tokyo Toronto Warsaw

with associated companies in Berlin Ibadan

Oxford is a registered trade mark of Oxford University Press
in the UK and in certain other countries

British Library Cataloguing in Publication Data available

Hardback ISBN 0-19-910814-5
Paperback ISBN 0-19-910815-3

1 3 5 7 9 10 8 6 4 2

Printed in Hong Kong

Picture acknowledgements
7 N.H.P.A./Anthony Bannister; 8 Natural History Museum, London;
9 Oxford Museum of Natural History; 10 Natural History Museum, London;
16 Natural History Museum, London; 17 TR Natural History Museum, London;
17 BR Natural History Museum, London; 22 Natural History Museum, London;
24 Natural History Museum, London; 27 Natural History Museum, London;
29 Universal/Courtesy Ronald Grant Archive; 33T Natural History Museum, London;
41TR Natural History Museum, London; 41BR Natural History Museum, London

All artwork © Steve Kirk except the following:
Jim Channell: 22bl, 23bl, 34b; Tessa Eccles: 13c, bl, br; European Map Graphics: 11br;
Denys Ovenden: 14tr, 30tr; Oxford Scientific Films/Steve Kirk:11, 30-31, 32-33, 33bl, 36-37;
Paul Richardson: 13t, 18t; Terry Riley: cover, 10l, 26l, 39br, 41l;
Chris Tomlin: 7tl, 25tr, 27tr, 33br; Jenny Williams: 9br, 20br, 37tr

OXFORD
First Book
of
Dinosaurs

Contents

What is a dinosaur?   6

How do we know about dinosaurs?   8

Dinosaur worlds   10

How dinosaurs lived

Big and small   12

Fast and slow   14

Meat-eaters   16

Plant-eaters   18

Defence   20

Displaying dinosaurs   22

Eggs, nests and young   24

Dinosaur groups

Tyrannosaurus rex   26

Dromaeosaurs   28

Stegosaurs and Ankylosaurs   30

Triceratops   32

Maiasaura   34

Brachiosaurus   36

Could dinosaurs fly or swim?   38

The end of the dinosaurs   40

Dinosaur detective quiz   42

Glossary   44

Dinosaur names   46

Index   47

What is a dinosaur?

The name 'dinosaur' means 'terrible lizard'. Dinosaurs were given their name because they look a bit like the lizards alive today. But dinosaurs died out 65 million years ago, and they were different from lizards and other living reptiles. They could walk on straight legs tucked under their bodies, instead of out at the side. This meant they could walk further, move faster and grow bigger than any other reptiles.

▶ Some dinosaurs, like this *Allosaurus*, walked on two strong legs and used their arms for grasping. Their long tails helped them to balance.

Dinosaur groups

There were over a thousand different kinds of dinosaur. They all developed from a single ancestor, about 230 million years ago. There were two main groups, each with a different shape of hip. Yet all dinosaurs had certain things in common, such as a scaly skin and laying eggs with shells. They all lived on land, and none of them could fly.

Look Closer

The two dinosaur groups are bird-hipped and lizard-hipped. In lizard-hipped dinosaurs, the two lower hip bones point in opposite directions — one forwards and one backwards. In bird-hipped dinosaurs the two lower hip bones point in the same direction, which is backwards.

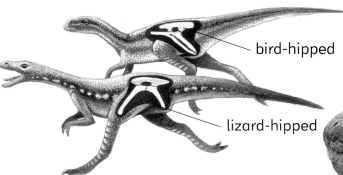

bird-hipped

lizard-hipped

▼ Most dinosaurs, like this *Iguanodon*, ate plants. Many stored plants in cheek pouches while they were busy chewing. There was no grass in dinosaur times, but plenty of leaves, fruit and roots to feed on.

Living relatives

Crocodiles have been around since before the time of the dinosaurs. Today they are the nearest living reptile relatives of dinosaurs. Some were powerful enough to kill the biggest plant-eating dinosaurs.

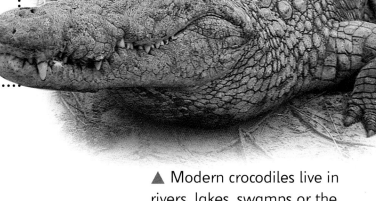

▲ Modern crocodiles live in rivers, lakes, swamps or the sea. But some ancient crocodiles lived on land, like the dinosaurs.

How do we know about dinosaurs?

No one has ever seen a living dinosaur. They died out millions of years before people walked on the Earth. Most of what we know about these amazing creatures comes from their bones, teeth and claws that have been preserved in the rocks as fossils.

▲ Living reptiles today, such as this iguana, can give scientists clues about what dinosaurs looked like and how they behaved. One dinosaur, *Iguanodon*, was even named after the iguana.

From dinosaur to fossil

When a dinosaur died, its soft flesh and skin was eaten by other animals or rotted away. Sometimes its hard parts, such as its bones, were buried quickly by mud or sand, which stopped them being broken up. Spaces in these hard parts filled up with rock or minerals, making a stone copy called a fossil. This did not happen very often, so dinosaur fossils are very rare.

▲ A dinosaur dies.

▲ Its bones are covered by sand and minerals fill the spaces in the bones, making rock.

▲ People may find the dinosaur bones when the rock over them wears away.

Putting the pieces together

Building a dinosaur from its fossil bones is a bit like doing a jigsaw puzzle – only some of the pieces are usually missing! Ridges, scars, holes and grooves on the bones show the positions of muscles, tendons, nerves and blood vessels. Fossil skulls even show how big dinosaur brains were. Footprints may show the shape of the foot, and skin prints the texture of the skin. Most dinosaurs had a scaly skin, often with bony plates set into it. We can only guess at the colour of the skin, based on the colour of the skin in living animals today.

◀ Scientists can bring a dinosaur back to life by fitting its bones together on a frame, then adding the muscles that moved the bones, and finally putting the skin on top. The real bones are usually too precious to use, so copies are made.

Activity

Try making your own fossils. You will need:
· plaster of Paris,
· modelling clay,
· shells or the bones from a cooked fish or chicken.

1. Roll out a thick layer of clay. Press the shell or bone firmly into the clay, then remove it, leaving a hollow shape.

2. Mix some plaster of Paris in an old jug and pour it into the hollow.

3. When your 'fossil' has set hard, you can paint or varnish it.

Dinosaur worlds

Dinosaurs lived on Earth for over 160 million years. (We humans have been here for about 2 million years so far.) During that time, the big areas of land called continents slowly moved apart, and the weather changed. This made the plants change too, and so did the dinosaurs.

Plants and animals

At the beginning of dinosaur times, the most common plants were ferns, horsetails, tree ferns, cycads and conifer trees. Later on, flowering plants appeared. Animal life on land included lizards, snakes, tortoises and crocodiles, as well as small furry mammals. Flying and gliding through the skies were reptiles called pterosaurs, and the first birds.

◀ The first dinosaurs lived about 230 million years ago, during a warm and sometimes dry period called the Triassic.

▼ This maidenhead or ginkgo tree was already around in the time of the dinosaurs.

▲ In Jurassic times, the warm and wet tropical conditions were ideal for dinosaurs. The giant long-necked dinosaurs, such as *Omeisaurus*, first appeared at this time.

▶ When the continents were joined together, dinosaurs could wander all over the world. As they drifted apart, dinosaurs were separated from each other. They began to develop into many new kinds, or species.

Triassic period 250–208 million years ago

Continents and climates

During the age of the dinosaurs, the continents slowly drifted apart. This movement affected the weather and climate. It was generally warm and dry all over the world at first, but it became slightly cooler and wetter later on, in Jurassic times. By Cretaceous times, the continents were roughly in the same positions they are in today. Climates grew drier, and seasons became more different in the northern and southern parts of the globe.

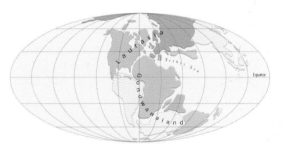

Jurassic period 208–144 million years ago

Cretaceous period 144–65 million years ago

Big and small

Can you imagine gigantic dinosaurs big enough
to reach the treetops? *Brachiosaurus* was this big.
Another huge dinosaur, *Diplodocus*, was as long as
three buses. These monsters must have made the
ground shake as they walked along. Even though
dinosaurs like these were some of the biggest,
heaviest and longest land animals of all time,
many other dinosaurs were
tiny. The smallest was
only as big as a chicken.

▶ When *Brachiosaurus*
stretched up its neck like a
giraffe, it stood 13 metres
tall. It weighed as much as
13 African elephants, and
ate the equivalent of 35
bales of hay every day.

Giant plant-eaters

The biggest dinosaurs of all were the long-necked plant-eaters called sauropods. They could feed at the tops of trees, which smaller dinosaurs could not reach. Inside their bodies were arched backbones, rather like bridges, that spanned the front and back legs. The long neck was built like a huge crane, with the neck bones forming the arm of the crane.

◄ Very strong bones helped to support the massive weight of *Brachiosaurus*. Its huge front legs were longer than the back legs, and they probably helped it reach up even higher for food.

▲ A modern elephant also has a very strong skeleton. But it is nothing like as big as the giant dinosaurs.

Small and clever

Many of the small dinosaurs were agile, clever meat-eaters. These lightweight hunters were no bigger than a child. They darted about on their two skinny legs, grabbing lizards and mouse-sized mammals with their small arms and sharp teeth. Other small dinosaurs, such as *Anchisaurus* and *Pisanosaurus*, were plant-eaters.

▼ *Anchisaurus* was an early type of long-necked plant-eater. But at 2.4 metres long, it was more than ten times smaller than *Brachiosaurus*!

▲ *Pisanosaurus* was about the same weight as a pet cat. This small, plant-eating dinosaur was alive at the same time as the first meat-eating dinosaurs, such as *Eoraptor*.

Fast and slow

Most of the larger dinosaurs plodded along slowly, usually not much faster than a person walking. If they had tried to run, they would have broken their bones. Medium-sized dinosaurs, such as *Triceratops*, may have trotted quite fast. Some of the smaller dinosaurs, such as *Hypsilophodon*, could run almost as fast as a galloping racehorse.

▼ *Triceratops* could probably trot as fast as a rhinoceros does today.

Slow and steady

The giant dinosaurs, such as *Diplodocus* and *Apatosaurus*, had to move on four legs to support their great weight. They strolled around at speeds of four to six kilometres per hour, and were simply too heavy to run. Other dinosaurs could move slowly on all-fours, but run faster on two legs to escape danger. Dinosaur footprints show that dinosaurs sometimes marched long distances in huge herds. Perhaps they had to move to find food or warmer climates in winter.

Look Closer

Scientists have worked out how fast dinosaurs moved by looking at their footprints, which have been preserved in the rocks. If the footprints are close together, the dinosaurs were walking slowly. If they are far apart, they were moving faster.

Speedy dinosaurs

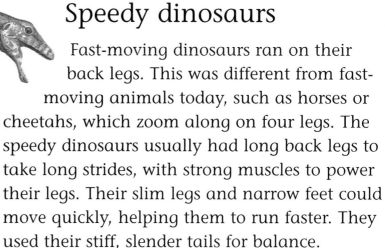

Fast-moving dinosaurs ran on their back legs. This was different from fast-moving animals today, such as horses or cheetahs, which zoom along on four legs. The speedy dinosaurs usually had long back legs to take long strides, with strong muscles to power their legs. Their slim legs and narrow feet could move quickly, helping them to run faster. They used their stiff, slender tails for balance.

Speed was useful to these dinosaurs for two main reasons. It helped them to catch their prey, and to escape from attack. Fast-moving dinosaurs included *Gallimimus*, *Compsognathus* and *Heterodontosaurus*. Some of them could reach speeds of 56 kilometres per hour.

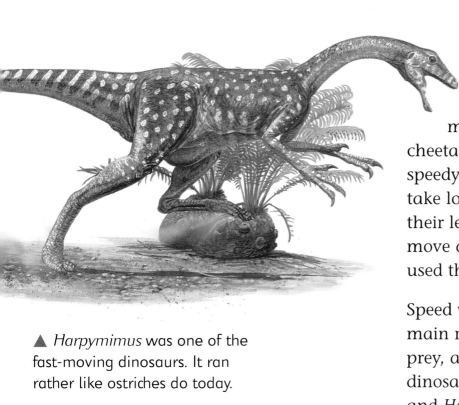

▲ *Harpymimus* was one of the fast-moving dinosaurs. It ran rather like ostriches do today.

▼ Speedy *Hypsilophodons* dart about under the lumbering feet of a herd of *Diplodocus*.

Meat-eaters

Armed with stabbing teeth and sharp claws, meat-eating dinosaurs were fierce predators. They all had short, muscular bodies, strong back legs, thin arms and low, powerful tails. They ate every kind of meat – insects, lizards, frogs, mammals and even other dinosaurs! Some were cannibals, eating dinosaurs of their own kind.

▲ *Tyrannosaurus rex* was one of the biggest meat-eaters ever to walk the Earth. Its jaws were so big that it could have swallowed a person whole.

Look Closer

Meat-eating dinosaurs needed good eyesight and to be clever enough to plan an attack, so they had larger brains than plant-eating dinosaurs. *Troodon* had a bigger brain for its body size than almost any other dinosaur.

partly forward-facing eyes helped *Troodon* to judge distance and pounce on prey

alert, bird-like head

Huge and hungry

The biggest meat-eaters, such as *Tyrannosaurus*, had huge heads, with curved teeth that had rough edges. They probably ran up to their prey and bit off huge chunks of flesh. These dinosaurs could not chew their food, so they swallowed it whole. They needed to eat a lot of meat to keep going. They may have stolen meals from other meat-eaters, and eaten dead animals as well as live ones.

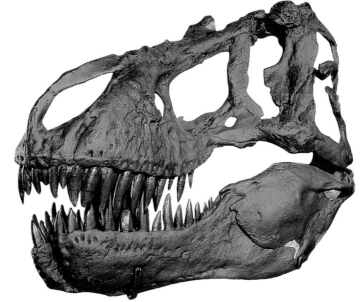

▲ Holes in the skull bones of a *Tyrannosaurus* helped to keep its huge head light, so it was not too heavy to lift and move.

Utahraptor

Deinonychus

Velociraptor

◀ *Deinonychus* hunted in packs, like wolves do today. It could catch and kill dinosaurs much bigger than itself.

Small but deadly

The small and medium-sized meat-eating dinosaurs like *Utahraptor*, *Baryonx*, *Velociraptor* and *Deinonychus* were more nimble. They had long, grasping arms and hands and long, narrow jaws. They could run fast, to catch mammals and insects.

▶ *Baryonyx* used the huge hook-like claws on its hands to spear prey, such as fishes.

Plant-eaters

From the giant long-necked sauropods and the armoured dinosaurs, to the horned and duckbilled dinosaurs, most dinosaurs ate plants. We can tell what sort of plants they ate from the fossils of plants that grew when they were alive, and from fossils of their droppings.

▶ Many dinosaurs swallowed stones and kept them in their stomachs to help them grind up their food. Birds and crocodiles do this today.

▼ *Edmontonia* shredded low-growing plants with its small, ridged teeth. It had large cheek pouches in which to store food.

lung

kidney

small intestine

liver

large intestine

stones stored in a muscular sac called a gizzard.

Dinosaur food

There was no grass around in dinosaur times, but plenty of other plants grew in the warm, moist climate. Some of these plants still grow today. These include pine trees, ferns, horsetails and palm-like cycads. Flowering plants, such as magnolias, also developed towards the end of the dinosaurs' time on Earth, in Cretaceous times.

Types of teeth

Sauropods did not chew their food at all. They just nipped off leaves with their pencil-like teeth and swallowed them straight away. In the stomach, food was ground up by stones which they had also swallowed, or broken down by bacteria. Sauropods had to eat masses of plants to get enough energy to survive.

▼ *Brachiosaurus* had sharp teeth to nip new leaves, cones and fruit from the tops of the trees. It could reach up to 13 metres — much higher than any other sauropod.

▶ The duckbilled dinosaur *Anatotitan* had hundreds of sharp teeth in tightly-packed rows. They chopped up plants like a vegetable grater. As its old teeth wore out, new ones grew to replace them.

The duckbilled dinosaurs had lots of sharp teeth to grind and chop up their food before they swallowed it. They also had cheek pouches, like hamsters, so they could store food and chew it properly later on. Dinosaurs like *Triceratops* ate very tough plants, such as cycads and pine trees. They had very powerful jaws and scissor-like teeth to cope with them.

Defence

Plant-eating dinosaurs had to defend themselves from meat-eating dinosaurs and other predators. Some used camouflage or speed to escape from danger. Other dinosaurs were well protected by plated skin like a suit of armour, tail spikes, tail clubs or sharp horns on the head.

 The tail of a *Scolosaurus* ended in twin spikes. When it swished its tail to the side the tip moved fast and could cause great damage.

▶ A predator could never bite through the bony plates covering the whole body of this *Saichania*.

Armoured tanks

Just like soldiers sheltering inside an army tank, the armoured dinosaurs were safe inside their tough, spiky, armour-plated skins. Some of them also had vicious spikes or heavy bony clubs on the end of their tails. They would swing their tails to drive the spikes or clubs into an enemy.

Activity

Try making an armoured dinosaur such as *Saichania*, *Ankylosaurus*, *Euoplocephalus* or *Sauropelta*.
You will need:
- modelling clay,
- a plastic comb or a pine cone,
- small pebbles or marbles,
- large, flat seeds
  (such as pumpkin seeds).

1. Make the basic shape out of modelling clay — a long body, four short stout legs, a long tail and a small head.

2. Push some teeth from the comb or some pine cone scales into the clay to make spikes and plates.

3. Push the seeds into the clay to represent the dinosaur's scales.

4. Make a tail club out of the small pebbles or marbles.

Whiplash tails

The giant sauropods were too big to have many enemies, but would use their tails to lash out sharply if they were attacked. At the end of the long, heavy tail was a thin, bendy tip, which would lash like a whip.

▼ *Hypselosaurus* had a whiplash tail like that of *Diplodocu*s, although it was smaller. Its body was about 12 metres long.

Horns and spines

Some dinosaurs had massive horns on the head and bony neck frills or spines on the neck. A neck or head wound could quickly kill a dinosaur, so it was important to have extra protection for this part of the body.

▶ *Sauropelta's* long, sharp neck spines and armoured skin helped to keep it safe from predators such as *Deinonychus*.

Displaying dinosaurs

Male and female dinosaurs often looked different from each other. The males had larger horns and crests. They may have used these to show off to the females, to fight for females, or to claim a territory.

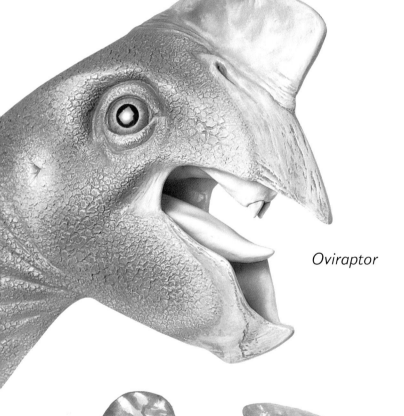

Oviraptor

▲ Male horned dinosaurs, like this *Brachyceratops*, may have used their horns to fight other males for the right to live and feed in their own area, called their territory.

◄ The crests of male *Oviraptors* and male duckbills such as *Corythosaurus* and *Parasaurolophus* may have been covered with coloured skin to help them to attract females.

Musical crests

The crests on the heads of duckbilled dinosaurs were different in males and females, and in their young. Each species of duckbill also had a different crest. The crests were hollow, and by puffing out hard these dinosaurs could have made loud hooting or trumpeting sounds through them. These sounds probably helped them to stay in touch with other members of their group. Males could also bellow a challenge to other males.

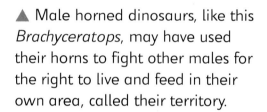

Corythosaurus   *Parasaurolophus*

▲ The sail of an *Ouranosaurus* was made from skin stretched over spines sticking up from the backbone.

Mystery sail

Ouranosaurus may have used the large sail along its back to attract a mate, rather like a male peacock uses its tail feathers today. Or perhaps a male with a bigger sail might have scared off a rival with a smaller sail by looking bigger and stronger. Another idea is that the sail might have acted as a sort of radiator, to help *Ouranosaurus* warm up or cool down.

Thick heads

Pachycephalosaurs, or thick-headed dinosaurs, had a thick layer of bone on top of their skull, rather like a built-in crash helmet. Males probably crashed their heads together in fights to win females. But their bony helmets also protected their soft brains from damage. Bighorn sheep fight in the same way today, and they have thick skulls too.

▲ *Prenocephale* also had a rigid, strong helmet.

◀ Two male *Pachycephalosaurus* have a head-butting contest. Their helmets were up to 25 cm thick, and their backbones and hip bones were strengthened to absorb the impact of their crashes.

Eggs, nests and young

Dinosaurs laid their eggs in a nest of soil and leaves on the ground. They would lay 10 to 30 eggs at a time. They may even have sat on the nest, to keep the eggs warm and protect them. Some baby dinosaurs could fend for themselves as soon as they hatched. Others had to be cared for by their parents.

▼ These baby *Orodromeus* have just hatched out of their eggs and are ready to leave the nest straight away.

Small eggs

Dinosaur eggs were not nearly as big as you might expect. They were never much larger than a football. If they had been bigger they would have needed thicker shells to stop them collapsing, and these thick shells would not have allowed enough air through to the babies. The babies also could not have broken out of really thick shells to hatch. The eggs often had lumps and bumps on the surface to stop them from packing together too tightly.

◄ At least two meat-eaters, including these *Oviraptor* and another dinosaur called *Troodon*, laid eggs.

Bringing up baby

As far as we can tell, some dinosaurs were good parents, protecting their young rather like crocodiles do today. Lots of duckbill dinosaur nests have been found in one place, showing that these dinosaurs nested together for protection. Baby duckbills had very wobbly legs, so they had to stay in the nest and eat soft plants brought by their parents.

Other baby dinosaurs could trot about and find scraps of food as soon as they hatched. When they were old enough to travel with a herd of adults, the young walked in the middle of the group, so that they were protected by the adults around them.

▼ A mother *Orodromeus* watches over her young. If the young dinosaurs stick together, they have many pairs of eyes and ears to watch out for danger.

Look Closer

Inside an eggshell, a developing dinosaur floated inside a bag of fluid, which cushioned it from knocks. It fed on the special, high-protein food stored in a yolk sac, and breathed air that seeped in through the shell.

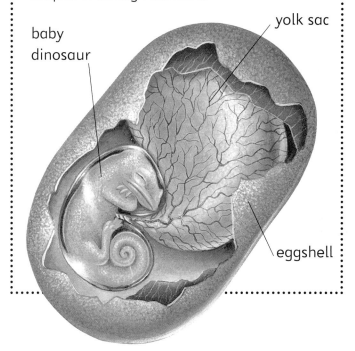

baby dinosaur

yolk sac

eggshell

Tyrannosaurus rex

Tyannosaurus rex and its relatives all had a massive head and a huge body, supported by two large back legs, which ended in three toes. A long, powerful tail helped them to balance when they walked upright.

Tyrannosaurus rex

Taller than a double-decker bus and heavier than an elephant, *Tyrannosaurus rex* may have hidden in wait for its prey, suddenly charging at them with its mouth wide open. Its razor-sharp teeth would have pierced a dinosaur's thick skin, then it might have twisted its head to and fro to rip out a chunk of flesh. *T.rex* probably also fed on dead animals, which had been killed by other dinosaurs.

◀ The name *Tyrannosaurus rex* means 'tyrant lizard king'. A tyrant is a cruel king.

Look Closer

Tyrannosaurus's arms were so short they did not even reach its mouth, so what use were they? They may have helped the dinosaur push itself upright after lying down. *Tyrannosaurus's* head was also very heavy, so if its arms had been large and heavy too, it would have found it difficult to balance upright on two legs. This is how it may have got up:

1

2

3

4

▲ The saw-edged teeth of a *Tyrannosaurus rex* were as long as knives. They curved backwards to give a good grip on a victim.

▶ *Acrocanthosaurus* had a ridged back because its spines were covered with skin. Its name means 'tall-spined lizard'.

Acrocanthosaurus

Another giant hunter that lived in North America just before *T.rex* was called *Acrocanthosaurus*. It was a similar shape to *T.rex* and about the same length, but was two metres shorter in height and lighter. *Acrocanthosaurus* was a large and terrifying meat-eater, which might have eaten sauropods.

Dromaeosaurs

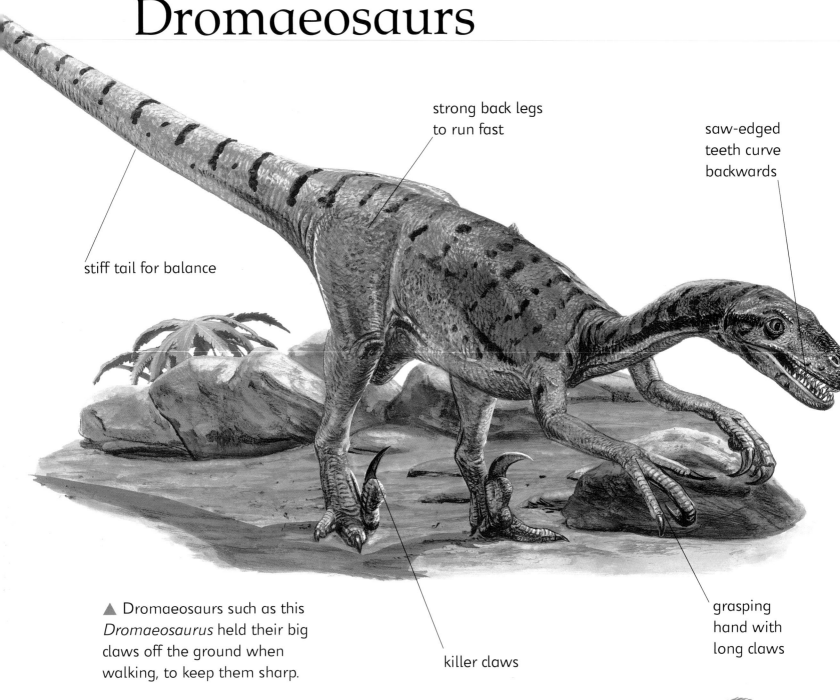

strong back legs
to run fast

saw-edged
teeth curve
backwards

stiff tail for balance

▲ Dromaeosaurs such as this
Dromaeosaurus held their big
claws off the ground when
walking, to keep them sharp.

killer claws

grasping
hand with
long claws

With great curved claws on their feet
and teeth like daggers, dromaeosaurs
were terrifying predators. These small,
swift dinosaurs had powerful jaws,
strong arms and big brains, which
helped them to plan their attacks.
Dromaeosaurs include dinosaurs such
as *Dromaeosaurus*, *Deinonychus*, *Utahraptor*
and *Velociraptor*.

Dromaeosaurus

As tall as a ten-year-old child and weighing as much as a large turkey, *Dromaeosaurus* was a small, fierce meat-eater. It probably leapt on its prey, flicking its claws forwards and slashing the flesh with its terrible talons. Its head was light so it could move it about quickly to grab prey. *Dromaeosaurus* may have eaten lizards, turtles and baby dinosaurs.

▶ *Deinonychus* probably hunted in packs, like wolves or hunting dogs do today, so it could attack animals much larger than itself.

▶ *Velociraptor* means 'fast thief', and it had long, slender legs for fast running. It attacked dinosaurs such as *Protoceratops*.

Deinonychus

Deinonychus means 'terrible claw'. This dinosaur had a vicious claw on the second toe of each back foot. When attacking large dinosaurs, *Deinonychus* probably balanced on one foot and kicked out with the other to slash open the soft belly of its prey. It used its stiff, bony tail to balance as it leapt.

Stegosaurs and Ankylosaurs

Tough, chunky dinosaurs, such as *Stegosaurus* and *Minmi*, were well protected by bony studs, plates or spikes along their backs or tails. They probably ate low-growing plants, chewing them with their small, weak teeth. Stegosaurs developed first, in Jurassic times. Later on, in the Cretaceous period, they were mostly replaced by ankylosaurs.

▲ *Euoplocephalus* was a typical ankylosaur, armoured from head to foot with a heavy, bony tail club to swing at predators. It even had bony eyelids, to protect its eyes.

Why did stegosaurs have plates?

The two rows of bony plates along the backs of stegosaurs make them easy to recognise. The plates were fixed in the thick skin, not joined to the bones. They may have been used to soak up or give off heat. If a stegosaur pumped a lot of blood into its plates, they would have turned red. This could have startled an enemy, or attracted a mate.

▶ Even though *Stegosaurus* was as long as a bus, its brain was as small as a walnut. But it was big enough to help *Stegosaurus* survive for over 10 million years.

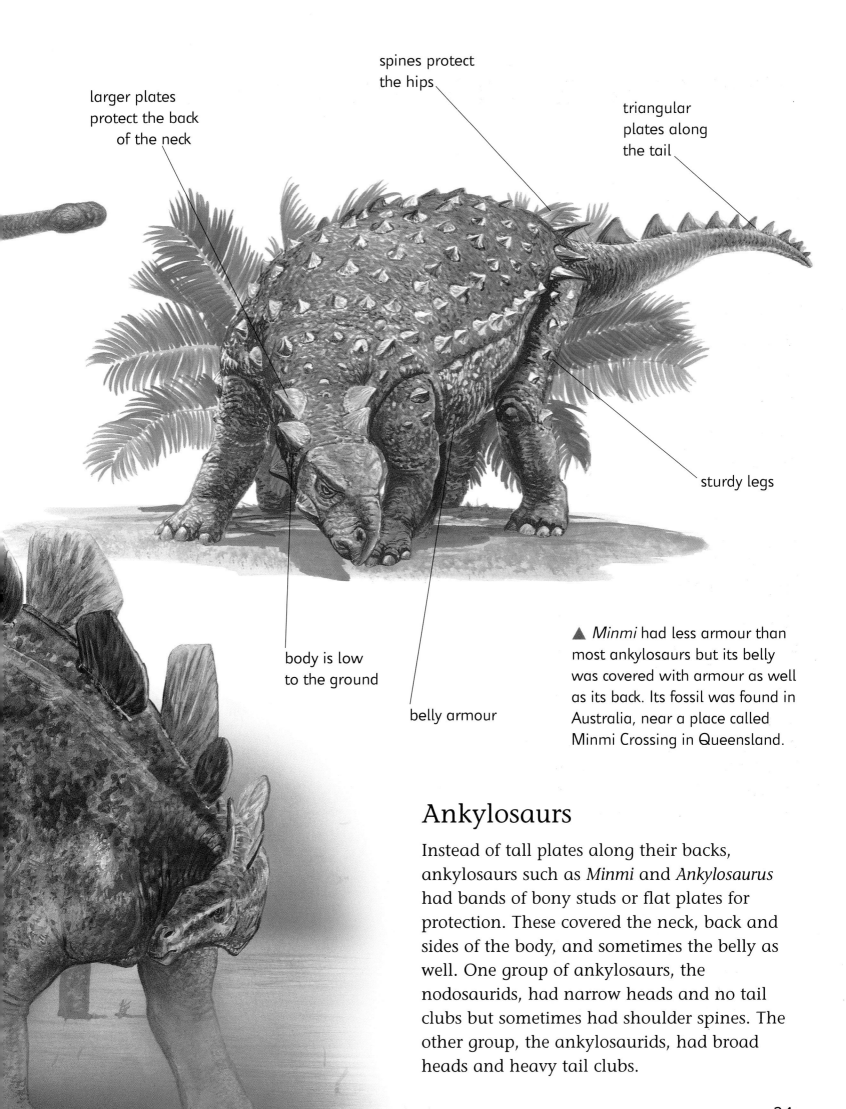

larger plates
protect the back
of the neck

spines protect
the hips

triangular
plates along
the tail

sturdy legs

body is low
to the ground

belly armour

▲ *Minmi* had less armour than
most ankylosaurs but its belly
was covered with armour as well
as its back. Its fossil was found in
Australia, near a place called
Minmi Crossing in Queensland.

Ankylosaurs

Instead of tall plates along their backs,
ankylosaurs such as *Minmi* and *Ankylosaurus*
had bands of bony studs or flat plates for
protection. These covered the neck, back and
sides of the body, and sometimes the belly as
well. One group of ankylosaurs, the
nodosaurids, had narrow heads and no tail
clubs but sometimes had shoulder spines. The
other group, the ankylosaurids, had broad
heads and heavy tail clubs.

Triceratops

Triceratops was the largest of the horned dinosaurs, and lived at the end of dinosaur times. As well as three horns, *Triceratops* had a large, bony frill over its neck and a narrow, hooked beak to snip off plants. Males used their horns for fighting, and displayed their frills to decide which animal should lead the herd.

▼ These dinosaurs probably lived in herds, so they could help each other fight off meat-eaters such as *Tyrannosaurus rex*.

Neck frills

The neck crest of *Triceratops* is unusual because it is made of solid bone. Other horned dinosaurs had holes in the middle of their crests, to make them less heavy. Perhaps they were used for recognising a mate or a member of the same species, or for showing how important an animal was in a herd.

▼ The huge skull of a *Triceratops* took up more than one third of its whole body length. Its head was as long as the height of a person.

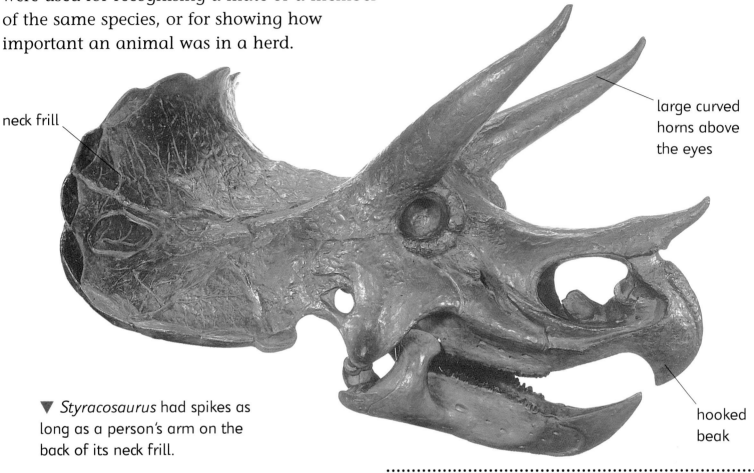

neck frill

large curved horns above the eyes

hooked beak

▼ *Styracosaurus* had spikes as long as a person's arm on the back of its neck frill.

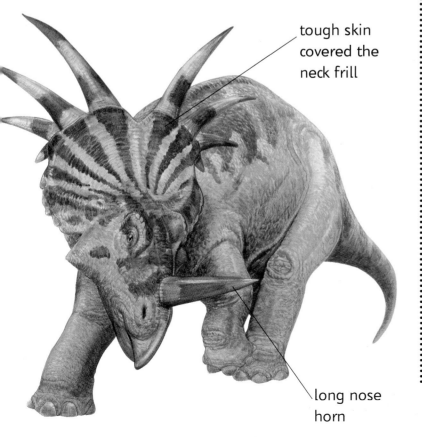

tough skin covered the neck frill

long nose horn

Look Closer

There are two main groups of horned dinosaurs. The first, such as *Chasmosaurus*, had a long neck frill, long horns above their eyes and a short nose horn. The second, such as *Centrosaurus*, had shorter frills, small eye horns and a large nose horn – rather like a rhinoceros.

Chasmosaurus   *Centrosaurus*

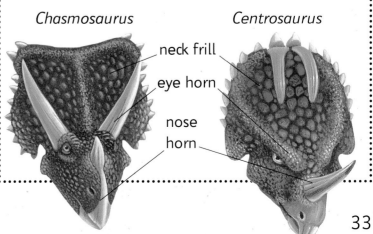

neck frill

eye horn

nose horn

33

Maiasaura

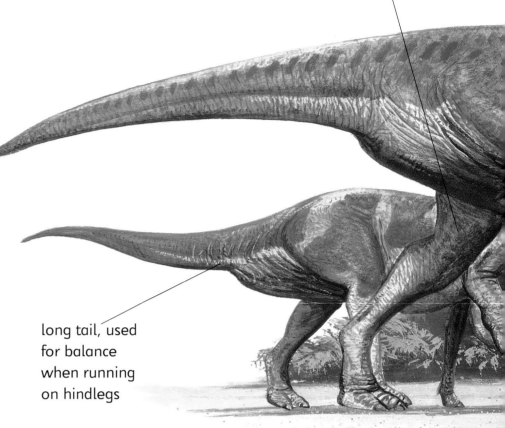

strong back legs

long tail, used for balance when running on hindlegs

The wide mouth of *Maiasaura* looks like a duck's beak, which is why dinosaurs like this are called duckbilled dinosaurs. They scooped up large mouthfuls of plants with their beaks, and chewed their food with rows of sharp cheek teeth. Many duckbills had large crests on their heads, but *Maiasaura* had only a low ridge.

Mother and baby

The name *Maiasaura* means 'good mother lizard'. Skeletons of *Maiasaura* were found with nests, babies and young ones, so it seems that they looked after their young. Nests were found one on top of the other, which suggests that female *Maiasaura* came back to the same nest site year after year, like some birds do today.

▲ *Maiasaura* probably lived in huge herds made up of many thousands of dinosaurs. As the seasons changed, the herds may have moved north and south to find the best food to eat.

Look Closer

Duckbills were noisy dinosaurs. Stretchy skin on the nose, or hollow crests on the head worked like echo chambers to make their hoots and bellows louder.

Saurolophus had a large head with a pointed crest.

Kritosaurus had a nose sac like a frog's stretchy throat pouch.

solid ridge
on head

wide beak
with no teeth

smaller front legs

No crests

Another dinosaur in the same group as
Maiasaura is *Anatotitan*. It too has no
crest, but it has a longer head and
long legs – rather like a horse.
Because *Anatotitan* was large, its
body probably worked at a slower
rate than those of smaller
dinosaurs. This may have helped
it to survive when there was a lot
of competition for food. *Anatotitan*
could live on low quality food, such
as ferns and pine needles.

▼ *Anatotitan* used its
tough jaws and wide
mouth to pick and chew
tough plants.

Brachiosaurus

The really big dinosaurs, such as *Argentinosaurus*, *Brachiosaurus* and *Diplodocus* all had small heads, long necks, bulky bodies and long tails. With their long necks they could reach a variety of plants at different heights so did not need to move too far each day. Many of these dinosaurs lived in herds, keeping the young in the middle of the herd for safety.

Why so big?

There are many advantages to being big. Giants are hard to attack, so the huge size and weight of the long-necked dinosaurs would have protected them against predators. Their large bodies also had space for a very long gut. This helped them to hold lots of plant food inside their bodies while they broke it down to release the goodness.

▼ *Riojasaurus* belongs to a group of dinosaurs called prosauropods, which may have been ancestors of the sauropods. They looked rather like sauropods, but some were fairly small.

Activity

Find out how stomach stones helped the sauropods to grind up their food.

You will need:
- a large yogurt pot with a lid,
- a large handful of lettuce leaves,
- a few small pebbles,
- water,
- two clear bowls.

1. Put the lettuce leaves, water and pebbles into the yogurt pot. Put the lid on tightly and shake hard for a few minutes.

2. Take out the pebbles and tip the contents of the pot into one of the bowls.

3. Do the same thing again, but without the pebbles. Compare the two bowls. Can you see how the lettuce that was with the pebbles is more mashed up and the water is greener?

Brachiosaurus

The name of this dinosaur means 'arm lizard'. The bone in the top part of its arm was seven times longer than the one in your arm! The body of a *Brachiosaurus* was as long as a tennis court, but it had a tiny head and brain. Its skull bones were quite thin, with air spaces between them, which made the small head even lighter. Brachiosaurus could not support a heavy head at the top of such a long neck.

▲ If you stood next to a *Brachiosaurus*, you would hardly reach past its knees!

Could dinosaurs fly or swim?

Dinosaurs were creatures of the land, and they could not fly. Other reptiles called pterosaurs glided through the skies above them. It seems clear now that birds have developed from small flesh-eating dinosaurs, which would mean that there are flying relatives of the dinosaurs alive today! Dinosaurs could swim if they had to, but they did not live in the water. The rulers of the seas were other reptiles such as plesiosaurs, ichthyosaurs and crocodiles.

▼ *Kronosaurus* was the largest known pliosaur. Its skull was more than twice the size of *Tyrannosaurus rex*'s. The big pliosaurs hunted smaller plesiosaurs, ichthyosaurs and sharks.

Underwater reptiles

Swimming through the oceans while the dinosaurs walked over the land were groups of reptiles that died out millions of years ago. They had to breathe air from the surface, like whales do today. There were long-necked plesiosaurs, short-necked pliosaurs, and icthyosaurs, which looked like dolphins. These reptiles were not closely related to the dinosaurs, or to each other.

Cryptocleidus, a plesiosaur

Kronosaurus, a pliosaur

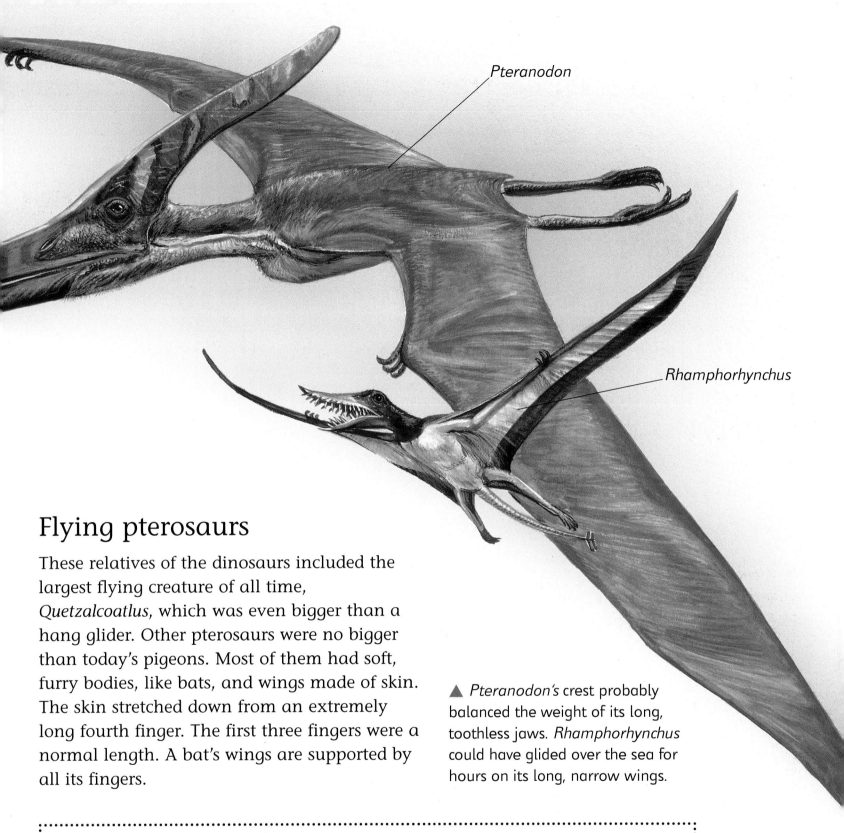

Pteranodon

Rhamphorhynchus

Flying pterosaurs

These relatives of the dinosaurs included the largest flying creature of all time, *Quetzalcoatlus*, which was even bigger than a hang glider. Other pterosaurs were no bigger than today's pigeons. Most of them had soft, furry bodies, like bats, and wings made of skin. The skin stretched down from an extremely long fourth finger. The first three fingers were a normal length. A bat's wings are supported by all its fingers.

▲ *Pteranodon's* crest probably balanced the weight of its long, toothless jaws. *Rhamphorhynchus* could have glided over the sea for hours on its long, narrow wings.

Look Closer

The shape of a pterosaur's head and teeth gives us clues about how it fed. The narrow, pointed head and long, forward-pointing teeth of *Rhamphorhynchus* (right) were ideal for catching fish. *Pterodaustro* had 2000 bristly teeth, for filtering small animals from the water.

teeth to hold slippery fish until they could be swallowed whole

The end of the dinosaurs

About 65 million years ago, the dinosaurs mysteriously died out. So did the flying pterosaurs, the swimming pliosaurs and some other reptiles and shellfish in the sea. No one knows for sure what happened to them. There may have been changes in climate, huge volcanic eruptions, or a gigantic comet or asteroid hitting the Earth, which made it impossible for the dinosaurs to survive.

▼ A meteorite hitting the Earth and volcanoes erupting would have thrown up huge clouds of dust and rocks and blocked out the warm Sun.

Disaster!

Scientists have found evidence of an enormous lump of rock from space – a meteorite – hitting the Earth in the Gulf of Mexico at the same time as the dinosaurs died out. Also at this time, India was pushing up against Asia, causing volcanoes to spew dust and poisons high into the air. Climates were becoming cooler, destroying some of the plants the dinosaurs ate and the places where they lived.

Mammals take over

When the dinosaurs died out, the mammals took over as rulers of the Earth. They developed from small, secretive creatures scurrying around feeding on insects, into the huge variety of mammals alive today – from mice and monkeys to tigers and elephants. Mammals' bodies are usually covered in fur or hair, unlike the dinosaurs' scales, and they give birth to babies instead of laying eggs.

▲ Tiny, furry mammals like this *Megazostrodon* lived alongside the first dinosaurs about 200 million years ago. Mammals survived when the dinosaurs died out.

◀ This early bird, called *Archaeopteryx*, has many features in common with dinosaurs. Small flesh-eating dinosaurs may have developed into birds over many millions of years.

▼ In the days of the dinosaurs, sea crocodiles were common. Today caimans like this one, and their relatives the crocodiles and alligators, live mostly in freshwater rivers and lakes.

The survivors

Many animals and plants were not wiped out with the dinosaurs. The survivors included crocodiles, lizards, turtles, snakes, mammals, birds, amphibians and most plants and sea creatures. Why did they survive? And why did so many other creatures die off all at the same time? Scientists have many different ideas for explaining this.

Dinosaur Detective Quiz

Now you can be a dinosaur detective, and track down the answers to this fun quiz. The dinosaurs are all in this book somewhere! Look for clues in the questions such as: the type of dinosaur (meat-eating, armour-plated...?); the size of dinosaur; the part of the body (teeth, claws...?); the topic (feeding, moving, eggs and babies...?) Then use the Contents list and the Index to help you find the right page. Good luck!

Can you find…?

- five dinosaurs that walked on two legs?
- three dinosaurs with huge claws?
- six dinosaurs with armour-plated skin?
- six meat-eating dinosaurs?
- six plant-eating dinosaurs?

Which…?

- Which dinosaur had a tail like a whip?
- Which dinosaurs had crash helmets?
- Which dinosaurs could fly?
- Which dinosaur was a long as three buses?
- Which dinosaur had a brain as small as a walnut?
- Which dinosaur had three horns on its head?
- Which living animals may be descended from the dinosaurs?

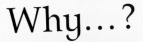

Why…?

- Why did sauropod dinosaurs have stones in their stomachs?
- Why did *T. rex* have short arms?
- Why has no-one ever seen a living dinosaur?
- Why did *Deinonychus* hunt in packs?
- Why did the dinosaurs die out?

How…?

- How did duckbilled dinosaurs get their name?
- How big were dinosaur eggs?
- How big was the smallest dinosaur?
- How did dinosaurs use their tails?
- How long were the teeth of *T. rex*?
- How tall was *Dromaeosaurus*?

Answers on page 48

Glossary

amniotic sac
A thin skin full of fluid that surrounds the developing embryos of reptiles, birds and mammals.

amphibian
An animal with a backbone that can live both in the water and on land. Frogs and newts are amphibians.

ankylosaur
A dinosaur with a broad head, bony armour on its back and a bony club on the end of its tail.

asteroid
A large lump of rock and iron out in space, which goes round and round the Sun. Some asteroids may hit planets like the Earth.

bacteria
A group of tiny living things made of one cell, which can only be seen through a microscope. Many bacteria are useful because they break down the remains of plants and animals.

camouflage
The way in which animals hide by using their colours, patterns or shapes to blend in with their surroundings.

cannibal
An animal that eats other members of its own species.

climate
The pattern of the weather over a long period of time.

conifer tree
A tree that produces its seeds in woody cones, such as a pine tree or a fir tree.

comet
A ball of frozen gas and dust that travels around the Sun. Some of the dust streams out from the comet to make a tail.

continent
One of the seven large areas of land on Earth, which are: Europe, Asia, Africa, North America, South America, Australia and Antarctica.

Cretaceous period
The time in the Earth's history, which lasted from 144 million years ago until 65 million years ago. The dinosaurs died out at the end of the Cretaceous period.

cycad
A plant with a thick trunk, long palm-like leaves and seeds in cones. Cycads were common in dinosaur times but are rare today.

dromaeosaur
A small, clever, fast-running dinosaur with large curved claws.

duckbilled dinosaurs
A large, plant-eating dinosaur with a beak like a duck. Many had crests on their heads. They lived in the Cretaceous period.

fossil
The remains of a plant or animal that once lived, usually preserved in rock.

gizzard
A bulge in the gut of some plant-eating dinosaurs with a tough, horny lining to grind up food. A gizzard has thick walls and lots of muscles.

horsetail
A swamp plant related to ferns that was more common when the dinosaurs were alive. Some grew as tall as trees, but today they are small, rare plants.

ichthyosaur
A reptile that lived in the sea when the dinosaurs lived on land.

intestine
A coiled tube leading from an animal's stomach to the hole where waste is pushed out of its body. In the intestine, or gut, food is broken down and goodness taken into the body.

Jurassic period
The time in the Earth's history which lasted from 208 until 144 million years ago. Large, plant-eating dinosaurs were common during this period.

mammal
A furry animal with a backbone that produces milk to feed to its young. People, mice, bats, horses and whales are all mammals.

meteorite
A big piece of rock or metal from space which falls down to Earth without burning up.

muscle
The 'meat' which joins onto bones and pulls them into different positions so that an animal can move.

pachycephalosaur
A plant-eating dinosaur with a thick dome of bone on the top of its skull.

plesiosaur
A large reptile that lived in the sea when the dinosaurs lived on land.

pliosaur
A plesiosaur with a short neck and a thick, powerful body.

predator
An animal that hunts and kills other animals for food.

prey
An animal that is killed by a predator for food.

pterosaur
A flying reptile that lived between 225 and 65 million years ago and was a distant relative of the dinosaurs.

reptile
A scaly animal with a backbone that lays eggs. Dinosaurs, pterosaurs, plesiosaurs and ichthyosaurs were all reptiles. Today's reptiles include crocodiles, snakes, lizards and turtles.

sauropod
A large, plant-eating, lizard-hipped dinosaur, with a long neck and a long tail, such as *Brachiosaurus* or *Diplodocus*.

species
A group of animals or plants that can breed with each other to produce young that can also breed. Members of a species usually look alike.

stegosaur
A dinosaur with a row of plates on its back and two pairs of long, sharp spikes at the end of its strong tail.

tendon
A tough sheet or thread which joins muscles to bones.

territory
The area in which an animal or a group of animals lives and which it defends fiercely against invaders.

Triassic period
The time in the Earth's history which lasted from 250 until 208 million years ago. The dinosaurs first appeared in the Triassic period.

volcano
An opening in the Earth's surface from which ash or hot, melted rock explodes. The ash and rock cool down to form a cone-shaped mountain.

Dinosaur names

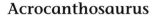

This list will help you to pronounce the names of the dinosaurs in this book.

Acrocanthosaurus
(a - crow - can - tho - **saw** - rus)

Allosaurus
(al - oh - **saw** - rus)

Anatotitan
(an - at - oh - **tie** - tan)

Anchisaurus
(**an** - key - **saw** - rus)

Ankylosaurus
(an - kylo - **saw** - rus)

Apatosaurus
(a - **pat** - oh - **saw** - rus)

Archaeopteryx
(ark - ee - **op** - ter - ix)

Argentinosaurus
(ar - gen - teen - oh - **saw** - rus)

Baryonyx
(barry - **on** - ix)

Brachiosaurus
(brack - ee - oh - **saw** - rus)

Brachyceratops
(brack - ee - **ser** - a - tops)

Centrosaurus
(**sen** - tro - **saw** - rus)

Chasmosaurus
(kaz - mo - **saw** - rus)

Compsognathus
(komp - sow - **nay** - thus)

Corythosaurus
(ko - rith - oh **saw** - rus)

Deinonychus
(die - **non** - i - kus)

Diplodocus
(dip - **lod** - oh - kus)

Dromaeosaurus
(**droh** - may - oh - **saw** - rus)

Edmontonia
(ed - mon - **tone** - ee - ah)

Eoraptor
(**ee** - oh - **rap** - tor)

Euoplocephalus
(you - oh - plo - **kef** - al - us)

Gallimimus
(gal - ee - **meem** - us)

Harpymimus
(**har** - pee - **meem** - us)

Heterodontosaurus
(**het** - er - oh - **dont** - oh - **saw** - rus)

Hypselosaurus
(**hip** - sel - oh - **saw** - rus)

Hypsilophodon
(hip - sil - **off** - oh -don)

Iguanodon
(ig - **wa** - no - don)

Kritosaurus
(**krite** - oh - **saw** - rus)

Maiasaura
(**my** - a - **saw** - ra)

Minmi
(min - **mi**)

Omeisaurus
(oh - **my** - ee - sa - us)

Orodromeus
(**or** - oh - **dro** - mee - us)

Ouranosaurus
(**oo** - ran - oh - **saw** - rus)

Oviraptor
(**oh** - vi - **rap** - tor)

Pachycephalosaurus
(pak - ee - **kef** - al - oh - saw - rus)

Parasaurolophus
(para - **saw** - row - **loaf** - us)

Pisanosaurus
(pee - **san** - oh - saw - rus)

Prenocephale
(pren - oh - **sef** - a - lee)

Protoceratops
(pro - toe - **ser** - a - tops)

Riojasaurus
(ree - **oh** - ha - **saw** - rus)

Saichania
(sigh - **chan** - ee - a)

Saurolophus
(**saw** - row - **loaf** -us)

Sauropelta
(**saw** - row - **pel** - ta)

Scolosaurus
(**sco** - low - **saw** - rus)

Stegosaurus
(**steg** - oh - **saw** - rus)

Styracosaurus
(sty - **rak** - oh - saw - rus)

Triceratops
(try - **serra** - tops)

Troodon
(**true** - oh - don)

Tyrannosaurus
(tie - **ran** - oh - **saw** - rus)

Utahraptor
(**you** - tah - rap - tor)

Velociraptor
(vel - **oh** - si - **rap** - tor)

Index

A
Acrocanthosaurus 27
alligator 41
Allosaurus 6
amniotic sac 25
amphibian 41
Anatotitan 19, 35
Anchisaurus 13
ankylosaur 30, 31
ankylosaurid 31
Ankylosaurus 20, 31
Apatosaurus 14
Archaeopteryx 41
Argentinosaurus 36
armoured dinosaurs 18,
  20–21, 30–31
arms 16, 17, 27, 28
asteroid 40

B
baby dinosaurs 24–25, 34
bacteria 19
balance 15, 26, 28,
  29, 34
Baryonyx 17
bat 39
beak 32, 33, 34, 35
bird 10, 18, 38, 41
bird-hipped dinosaurs 7
blood 9, 30
bones 8–9, 13, 14, 17,
  23, 33
Brachiosaurus 12, 13, 19,
  36–37
Brachyceratops 22
brain 9, 16, 28, 30

C
caiman 41
camouflage 20
cannibal 16
Centrosaurus 33

Chasmosaurus 33
claws 8, 16, 28, 29
climate 10–11, 40
comet 40
Compsognathus 15
conifer 10, 18, 19
continents 10–11
Corythosaurus 22
crested dinosaurs 22, 33, 34
Cretaceous period 11, 18, 30
crocodile 7, 10, 18, 38, 41
Cryptocleidus 38
cycad 10, 18, 19

D
defence 20–21
Deinonychus 17, 21, 28,
  29
diet 7, 13, 16–19, 39
digestion 18–19, 36, 37
Diplodocus 12, 14, 15,
  21, 36
dromaeosaur 28–29
Dromaeosaurus 28, 29
duckbilled dinosaurs 18, 19,
  22, 25, 34–35

E
Edmontonia 18
eggs 6, 24–25, 41
elephant 13
Eoraptor 13
Euoplocephalus 20, 30
extinction 40
eyes 16, 30

F
fern 10, 18
fighting 22, 23, 32
flight 38–39
footprints 14
fossils 8–9, 18

G
Gallimimus 15
ginkgo 10
gizzard 18, 37

H
hands 17, 28
Harpymimus 15
herds, living in 25, 32, 36
Heterodontosaurus 15
horned dinosaurs 18, 20, 21,
  22, 32–33
horsetail 10, 18
Hypselosaurus 21
Hypsilophodon 14, 15

I
ichthyosaur 38
iguana 8
Iguanodon 7, 8
intestines 18, 36

J
jaws 16, 17, 19, 28, 35
Jurassic period 11, 30

K
kidney 18
Kritosaurus 34
Kronosaurus 38

L
legs 6, 13, 14–15, 16, 26, 28,
  29, 31, 35
liver 18
lizard 10, 41
lizard-hipped dinosaurs 7
lung 18

M
magnolia 18
Maiasaura 34–35

Index

maidenhead tree 10
mammal 41
mating 22, 23, 33
meat-eaters 13, 16–17, 20, 24,
  26–27, 28–29, 32, 41
meteorite 40
Minmi 30, 31
movement 6, 14–15,
  17
muscles 9, 15

N
neck 13, 31, 36
neck frill 32, 33
necks 21
nerves 9
nests 24–25, 34
nodosaurid 31

O
Omeisaurus 11
Orodromeus 24–25
Ouranosaurus 23
Oviraptor 22, 24

P
pachycephalosaur 23
Pachycephalosaurus 23
Parasaurolophus 22
Pisanosaurus 13
plant-eaters 13, 18–19, 20,
  30–31, 34–35, 36–37
plants 10, 18, 41
plates 20–21, 30–31
plesiosaur 38
pliosaur 38, 40
predators and prey 16–17, 20,
  26–27, 28–29
Prenocephale 23
prosauropod 36
Protoceratops 29
Pteranodon 39

Pterodaustro 39
pterosaur 10, 38, 39, 40

Q
Quetzalcoatlus 39

R
reptile 6–7, 8, 38, 40
Rhamphorhynchus 39
Riojasaurus 36

S
Saichania 20
Saurolophus 34
Sauropelta 20, 21
sauropod 13, 18, 19, 21, 27,
  36–37
Scolosaurus 20
shark 38
skeleton 9, 13
skin 6, 9, 20–21, 30,
  33, 41
skull 9, 17, 23, 33, 38
snake 10, 41
stegosaur 30
Stegosaurus 30
stomach 18, 19, 37
Styracosaurus 33
swimming 38–39

T
tail 15, 16, 20, 21, 26, 28, 29,
  30, 31, 34, 36
teeth 8, 16, 17, 18, 19, 26, 27,
  28, 30, 34, 39
tendons 9
territory 22
toes 26, 29
tortoise 10
Triassic period 10, 11
Triceratops 14, 19, 32–33
Troodon 16, 24

turtle 41
Tyrannosaurus rex 16, 17,
  26–27, 32

U
Utahraptor 17, 28

V
Velociraptor 17, 28, 29
volcanoes 40

W
wings 39

Quiz answers

Can you find?
1 *Allosaurus, T. rex, Deinonychus, Oviraptor, Velociraptor, Utahraptor, Pisanosaurus*
2 *Deinonychus, Baryonyx, Dromaeosaurus, Harpymimus, Acrocanthosaurus, Utahraptor, Velociraptor, Oviraptor*
3 *Edmontonia, Saichania, Scolosaurus, Sauropelta*
4 *T. rex, Allosaurus, Dromaeosaurus, Baryonyx, Euoplocephalus, Minmi*
5 *Iguanodon, Triceratops, Brachiosaurus, Anchisaurus, Pisanosaurus, Hypselosaurus, Edmontonia, Anatotitan, Diplodocus*

Which?
1 *Diplodocus, Hypselosaurus*
2 *Pachycephalosaurus*
3 No dinosaurs could fly! But pterosaurs could...
4 *Diplodocus*
5 *Stegosaurus*
6 *Triceratops*
7 Birds

Why?
1 To help the grind up their food
2 To help it get up after lying down or to stop the front of its body being too heavy
3 Because dinosaurs died out millions of years before people were around
4 To help them catch animals larger than themselves
5 No one can be sure, but perhaps because of changes in climate, volcanic eruptions or a comet or asteroid hitting the Earth

How?
1 From their wide mouth, which looks like a duck's beak
2 Never much bigger than a football
3 As big as a chicken
4 For balance and for defence
5 As long as knives
6 As tall as a ten year old child